WITH

STRAWS

By Eiji Orii and Masako Orii   **Pictures by Kimimaro Yoshida**

Gareth Stevens Children's Books
Milwaukee

For a free color catalog describing Gareth Stevens' list of high-quality children's books, call 1-800-341-3569.

Library of Congress Cataloging-in-Publication Data

Orii, Eiji, 1909-
    Simple science experiments with straws / Eiji Orii and Masako Orii;
Kimimaro Yoshida (ill.). — North American ed.
        p. cm. — (Simple science experiments)
    Translated from the Japanese.
    Includes index.
    Summary: Presents experiments using straws, cards, and glasses to
demonstrate the pushing force of air.
    ISBN 1-55532-854-7 (lib. bdg.)
    1. Atmospheric pressure—Experiments—Juvenile literature.
[1. Atmospheric pressure—Experiments. 2. Experiments.] I. Orii,
Masako. II. Yoshida, Kimimaro, ill. III. Title. IV. Series.
QC885.O75   1989
507'.8—dc19   88-23298

North American edition first published in 1989 by

Gareth Stevens Children's Books
RiverCenter Building, Suite 201
1555 North RiverCenter Drive
Milwaukee, Wisconsin 53212, USA

This US edition copyright © 1989. First published as *Nihon No Sutoro (Let's Try Straws)* in Japan with an original copyright © 1987 by Eiji Orii, Masako Orii, and Kimimaro Yoshida. English translation rights arranged with Dainippon-Tosho Publishing Co., Ltd., through Japan Foreign-Rights Centre, Tokyo.

Additional text and illustrations copyright © 1989 by Gareth Stevens, Inc.

Series editor and additional text: Rita Reitci
Research editor: Scott Enk
Additional illustrations: John Stroh
Design: Laurie Shock

Technical consultant: Jonathan Knopp, Chair, Science Department, Rufus King High School, Milwaukee

Printed in the United States of America

3 4 5 6 7 8 9 96 95 94 93 92 91 90

Every day you go through air so easily that it does not seem as if there is anything at all to air. Sometimes we even call it "thin air."

But air has weight and force. Moving air is wind. Air takes up room. Air rushes into empty spaces. Air can push heavy things, or keep some things from moving at all.

With the help of drinking straws and some other everyday things, you can see for yourself some of the amazing things air can do.

Put a drinking straw in a glass of water and sip.

When you take away the air in the straw, the air pressing on the water in the glass outside the straw quickly forces some of the water up the straw to fill the empty space.

Will you get more water sipping through one straw or two?

You get more water through two straws.

You lower the air pressure in two straws. Air pushes from high pressure to low pressure. It pushes the water up both straws.

Now take one straw out of the glass and try to sip through both straws at once. What happens?

Only a little water comes up.

The air you take out of the first straw is at once replaced by air from the second straw. Water is not forced up the straw in the glass because the air pressure is the same in the straw as on the water.

What happens when you put your fingertip over the end of the straw that is out of the glass?

Now water comes up easily, just as when you used only one straw.

Try this with straws of different sizes.

Now let's try this with three straws. Put two straws in the glass and one outside the glass. Then sip. What happens?

If you put your fingertip over the end of the straw and sip, what happens?

Now see what happens when you leave one straw in the glass and put the other two outside.

Put your fingertip over the end of one of those straws and then sip. What happens?

Try covering the ends of both straws and sipping. What happens? For water to move, air must be able to push it.

Fill a soda bottle with water up to the top. Put a straw in the bottle and plug up the rest of the opening with clay or putty. Be sure no air can get through the plug. Can you sip water through the straw?

No, you can't. There is no air in the bottle to push the
water up the straw.

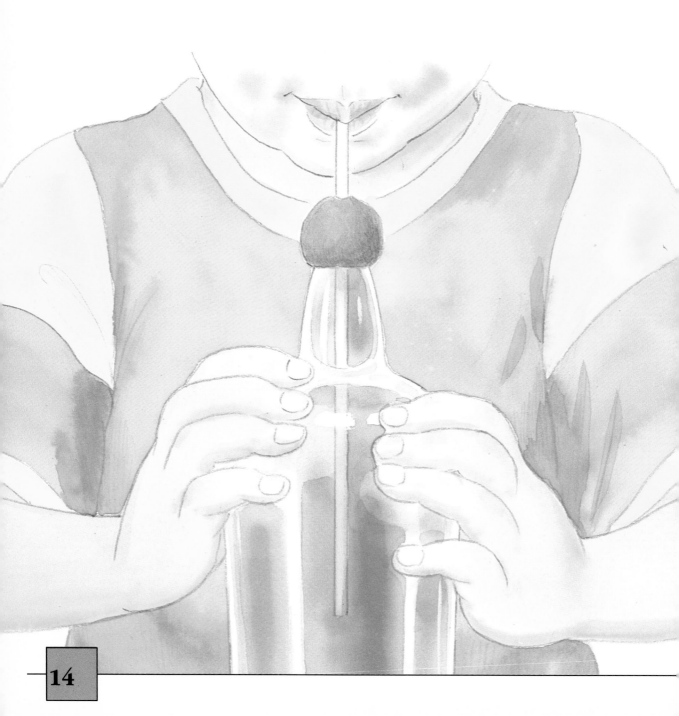

Find out what happens when you sip on two straws, one in the bottle and one outside.

The water still can't come up.

Now put the two straws in the bottle and carefully seal the opening with clay or putty. What happens when you sip on both straws?

Try sipping on only one straw. Does the air coming through the second straw push the water up?

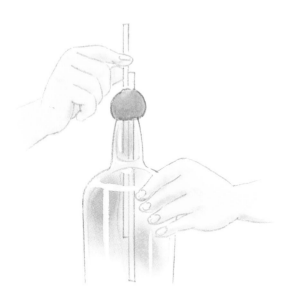

17

Try this over a sink. Fill a glass with water, put a postcard on the glass, and hold it in place with your hand. Now turn the glass upside down and let go of the postcard. What happens?

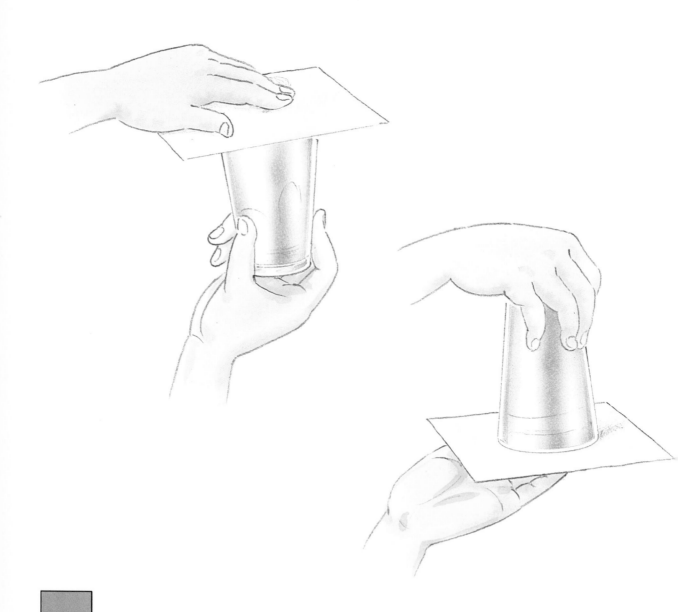

That's strange! The postcard doesn't fall. Why not? Can air get inside to help the water come out?

Let's see if holes will help. Be sure to do this over
the sink! Make a small hole in the postcard with a pin.
Then turn the glass upside down. Now let go of the
postcard. Did it stay, or did it fall?

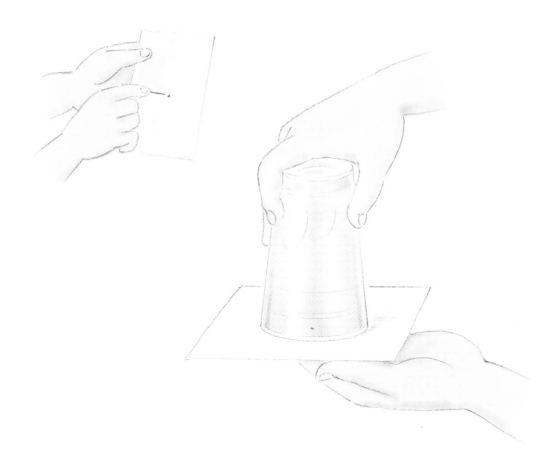

What happens when you make another small hole? Two
more holes?

Will lots of small holes let air in and water out?

In tiny holes, water forms a strong "skin" called surface tension. The air pressure against this surface tension is stronger than the weight of the water above. This air pressure holds up the postcard.

Now make larger holes. The bubbles show that air is getting inside the glass. Now the water can flow out, pushing away the postcard.

Using a can opener, make a very small hole in the top of a soda can close to the rim.

Now tip the can. Be sure to do this over the sink or a bowl!

Does the soda come out?

Now let's make another small hole in the can across from the first one.

This time, air can get in easily to push the soda out.

Pour out all the soda and put the can into a pail or a large bowl filled with water. Be careful not to bend the can as you hold it under the water. What happens?

Air comes out of the can because air is lighter than water.

Take the can out of the pail and pour from it. Did water go in to fill the space left by the air?

Now empty all the water out of the can. Put your finger over one of the holes and hold the can under water.

Do bubbles come out?
Not many.

Try to pour. Not much water gets into the can. Most of the air stays inside.

Can air push out and water push in through the same small hole at the same time?

When you do the experiment on page 18, the postcard does not drop. Let's see what happens when the glass is not quite filled with water.

Fill the glass almost to the top and put the postcard on it.

Hold the postcard on the top.

Turn the glass upside down.

Take away your hand. The postcard does not fall.

Now let's see what happens when there is no water at all in the glass.

This time the postcard falls!

What if the rim of the glass is wet?
Dip the rim of the glass in water.

Press the postcard firmly on the glass
so the water seals it around the rim.

Now turn the glass upside down
and let go of the postcard.

The postcard does not fall.
The air pressure outside the
glass is higher than inside
the glass. The water seal
keeps more air from getting
inside the glass.

A plastic goldfish "swims" inside two glasses full of water and placed mouth to mouth. You can make this happen, too.

Here's how.

Get two glasses of the same kind and size. Fill one up with water and put a plastic fish or another floating toy in it. Fill the second glass to the brim and put a postcard on it.

Turn the glass with the postcard upside down.

Set it on top of the other glass.

Keep the edges of the glasses close together while you pull out the postcard very carefully.

Now your plastic fish can "swim" happily in its aquarium!

GLOSSARY

Here is a list of words and phrases used in this book. After reading what the word or phrase means, you will see it used in a sentence.

air pressure: the weight of air against a surface. Higher air pressure means that the air is heavier than normal. Lower air pressure means that the air is lighter than normal.
At sea level, the normal air pressure is about 15 pounds per square inch.

brim: the topmost edge of a cup, glass, or bowl
She filled the glass to the brim.

experiment: a test, trial, or project
She did an experiment to learn about air pressure.

firmly: in a strong, steady way
She firmly held the bat as she waited for the ball.

plug: to stop up, or fill, a hole or a gap
Be sure to plug the sink before you wash the dishes.

rim: an edge or border of something
He swam to the rim of the pool.

seal: something that closes tightly to keep out air or water
His mother put a wax seal on each of the jars of jelly she made.

sip: to drink small amounts carefully
You have to suck the air when you sip through a straw.

straw: hollow stalks or stems of grain after the seeds have been removed; a single such stem used for drinking fluids; a drinking tube made of plastic, glass, waxed paper, or other material
He sipped his fruit juice through a straw.

surface tension: the strong invisible "skin" that forms over the surface of water
The surface tension let the insect run across the pond.

INDEX